S0-BIC-191

BASKETBALL OFFICIATING

The Barnes Sports Library

This library of practical sports books covers fundamentals, techniques, coaching and playing hints and equipment for each sport. Leading coaches and players have been selected to write these books, so each volume is authoritative and based upon actual experience. Photographs and drawings, or both, illustrate techniques, equipment and play.

ARCHERY
by Reichart & Keasey
BAIT CASTING
by Gilmer Robinson
BASEBALL
by Daniel E. Jessee
BASKETBALL
by Charles C. Murphy
BASKETBALL FOR GIRLS
by Meissner & Meyers
BASKETBALL OFFICIATING
by Dave Tobey
BETTER BADMINTON
by Jackson & Swan
BICYCLING
by Ruth & Raymond Benedict
BOWLING FOR ALL
by Falcaro & Goodman
BOXING
by Edwin L. Haislet
CHEERLEADING
by Loken & Dypwick
FENCING
by Joseph Vince
FIELD HOCKEY FOR GIRLS
by Josephine T. Lees
FLY CASTING
by Gilmer Robinson
FOOTBALL
by W. Glenn Killinger
FUNDAMENTAL HANDBALL
by Bernath E. Phillips
GOLF
by Patty Berg
HOW TO TIE FLIES
by E. C. Gregg
ICE HOCKEY
by Edward Jeremiah
JIU-JITSU
by Frederick P. Lowell
LACROSSE
by Tad Stanwick
LAWN GAMES
by John R. Tunis
PADDLE TENNIS
by Fessenden S. Blanchard
PHYSICAL CONDITIONING
by Stafford & Duncan
RIDING
by J. J. Boniface
RIFLE MARKSMANSHIP
by Lt. Wm. L. Stephens
ROLLER SKATING
by Bob Martin
ROPING
by Bernard S. Mason
SIX-MAN FOOTBALL
by Ray O. Duncan
SKATING
by Putnam & Parkinson
SKIING
by Walter Prager
SOCCER AND SPEEDBALL FOR GIRLS
by Florence L. Hupprich
SOCCER
by Samuel Fralick
SOFTBALL
by Arthur T. Noren
SOFTBALL FOR GIRLS
by Viola Mitchell
SWIMMING
by R. J. H. Kiphuth
TABLE TENNIS
by Jay Purves
TENNIS
by Helen Jacobs
TENNIS MADE EASY
by Lloyd Budge
TOUCH FOOTBALL
by John V. Grombach
TRACK AND FIELD
by Ray M. Conger
VOLLEY BALL
by Robert Laveaga
WRESTLING
by E. C. Gallagher

Clair Bee's Basketball Library

THE SCIENCE OF COACHING :: MAN-TO-MAN DEFENSE AND ATTACK
ZONE DEFENSE AND ATTACK :: DRILLS AND FUNDAMENTALS

BASKETBALL OFFICIATING

by

DAVE TOBEY

With a Foreword by

OSWALD TOWER

ILLUSTRATED

NEW YORK

A. S. BARNES AND COMPANY, INC.

PRINTED IN THE UNITED STATES OF AMERICA

DEDICATION

The author affectionately dedicates this volume to—

The late Dr. James Naismith, the gentle Y.M.C.A. physical instructor who invented the game.

Former top-flight officials who helped carry the torch for honest, intelligent officiating: Tom and Ed Thorpe, and Pete Synnott, deceased; John Wendelken, Edwin Hastings, John O'Brien, Frank Brennan, Arthur Carroll, John Murray, Ed Shaw, John Norton, Tom Degnan, Orsen Kinney, William Grieve and others too numerous to mention.

Contemporary officials who are helping carry on their work.

Dave Walsh, one of the greatest officials in the game until he retired to serve as Associate Director of the Officials Bureau. Eastern officials are now reaping the benefits of his sound advice and constructive criticism.

Ned Irish, who gave basketball a tremendous lift by placing it under ideal conditions at Madison Square Garden and by arranging local and intersectional contests before record crowds. These contests have helped promote a national uniformity of rules interpretation.

Asa S. Bushnell, Director of the Eastern Intercollegiate Association and the Officials Bureau, for his untiring efforts in improving the brand of officiating and in organizing clinics where coaches, players and officials may air their views.

Oswald Tower, editor of the rule book and official interpreter; Dr. John Brown, Jr., A. E. Metzdorf, and the various committees responsible for the Rule Book.

The coaches, graduate managers, and writers with whom the author has had 25 years of pleasant association. It has been his good fortune to meet the finest sportsmen in the country among these men.

PREFACE

FROM ITS HUMBLE beginnings 53 years ago, basketball has become the most popular of indoor games—the sport and fun of 10,000,000 players and 100,000,000 spectators.

It is unquestionably the fastest foot game on earth. And because of (1) the comparatively small playing area; (2) the lightning-swift changes from offense to defense, and vice-versa; (3) the prohibition of body contact; and (4) the complex playing code, it is perhaps the most difficult of all to officiate. In few other games does the official carry such a load and bear so directly upon the scoring.

Yet, despite the official's keystone function, little has been done to "improve the breed." Coaches snipe at the game administrators but offer little in the way of constructive criticism. Theirs is a strict hands-off policy. This is one of the reasons for the scarcity of capable arbiters.

Another is the lack of supervisory agencies, such as officiating or rating boards. Without such control, many officials relax their vigilance. They fail to familiarize themselves with the rules or with the principles of proper officiating procedure, lack a basketball background or fail to keep physically fit.

The officials certainly are not helped by sectional differences of interpretation. To suit its style of play, one section will adopt a certain interpretation that another will consider illegal. When representative schools meet, what is the official to do? Call them as *he* sees them and make at least one enemy, or hold a coaches' clinic before the game?

Leadership and guidance are very definitely needed. The purpose of this book is threefold:

1. To pass along to potential and practicing officials the fruits of the author's experience as player, coach and official.

2. To promote standardization and a better brand of officiating through an exposition of tested methods and techniques.

3. To supply material for clinical studies aimed at promoting better understanding of the rules and improved player-official and coach-official relationships.

DAVE TOBEY

CONTENTS

Preface vii
Foreword xi
1. Conditioning and Equipment 1
2. Ratings, Game Relationships, Ethics 7
3. Principles and Time Elements 12
4. Duties of the Single Official 16
5. The Double-Official System 23
6. Handling Game Situations 29
Screening 29
Fast Take-Outs 29
The "Bucket" 33
Dribbling 38
Rebounds 43
Out-of-Bounds 45
Jump Balls 53
Shooting 57
The Free Throw 59
7. Officiating on Non-Regulation Courts 62
8. Do's and Don'ts 65
Index 74

FOREWORD

THE OLDER GENERATION of basketball officials learned the duties of their profession and acquired their skill in the hard way. They were the pioneers; they graduated from the school of experience; they started from scratch and learned by trial and error. Experience is a good teacher and there is no substitute for it, but success is surer and more quickly attained when experience is supplemented by teachers who have traveled the road and who have themselves achieved success.

The great popularity of modern basketball is due in no small measure to the skill of the officials who administer the rules. Their task is one which demands thorough knowledge of the game and its rules, courage, honesty, keen observation, instantaneous decision and, above all, sound judgment. The nature of the game is such, and the demands upon those who administer it are so searching, that we marvel at the uniformity of officiating among the varied groups and many sections of which the complete basketball picture is composed.

A successful official who has given many years to the game, who has learned the duties of the profession through study, experience and association with other leading officials, has a fund of information on the subject. In this book Dave Tobey summarizes his rich experiences and offers sound instruction to aspiring basketball officials.

OSWALD TOWER.

BASKETBALL OFFICIATING

CODE OF SIGNALS

For Announcement of Fouls and Penalties by Officials

BLOCKING
hands on hips

RUNNING (WALKING)
rotating fists

10-SEC. RULE
Violation
arm raised clenched fist

HOLDING
grasping wrist

HELD BALL
thumbs up both hands

OUT OF BOUNDS
points direction of play and calls out name of team to receive the ball

PUSHING
arms pushing forward

NUMBER OF FREE THROWS FOR FOULS
right arm raised 1 or 2 fingers

NO BASKET
waving arms in front of body at hips

CHARGING
arms folded on chest

TIME OUT
sift hands before face
point to team taking time out

DOUBLE FOUL
arms extended palms front

HACKING
right hand chopping

3-SEC. RULE
Violation
arm raised
3 fingers showing

VIOLATION
right arm waves at waist line – thumb up.

HIPPING
right hand on hip

BASKET BALL

DISCONTINUED DRIBBLE
waving hand palm down

Drawn by J. Riegel, Jr.

Signals adopted by Collegiate Basketball Officials Bureau and Code printed by permission of that organization. Signals also used by Eastern Intercollegiate Basketball League.

Chapter 1

CONDITIONING AND EQUIPMENT

BASKETBALL OFFICIATING is the most difficult of all sports adjudicating tasks. The tremendous pace of the game, the lightning-like shifts from offense to defense, the complexity of the rules, and the fact that ten players are moving at high speed in a limited area where no body contact is permissible make the official's lot a most arduous one. There is no time to deliberate over a decision; the official must *think* in split-second time and *act* in practically the same instant.

The requisites of a good official, briefly, are: (1) Honesty. (2) Courage. (3) Efficient split-vision. (4) Physical fitness. (5) Good voice. (6) Firmness. (7) Business-like attitude. (8) Knowledge of the rules and techniques. (9) Common sense. (10) Sense of humor. (11) Poise.

CONDITION

It will be assumed here that you are the official. As the season approaches, your first physical concern will be condition. You owe it to yourself as well as to the players, coaches and spectators, to be in the best physical shape for every game.

Don't let the conditioning problem take care of itself; that is, work into condition as the season goes along. This isn't cricket. It is your duty to start the season in perfect condition. Stalling through the first few games reflects on your reputation.

It is a wise idea to get a medical checkup before, during, and after the season. Otherwise, common-sense health rules apply.

Condition yourself systematically and progressively. A month before the season, map out a program of walking, jogging, short sprints, and calisthenics to build your wind. Gradually increase these exercises and adapt them to game conditions; alternately jogging, walking, stopping, and speeding up.

After two weeks, you should be ready to transfer your training to the basketball court. Increase the workout time from fifteen minutes to one hour. Officiating practice games is a splendid conditioner. Several weeks of one-hour practice games will make the forty-minute regulation games seem easy.

Such training may be compared to over-distance work in track, where a miler will train by running two and three miles. Officials who finish a game in obvious distress cannot expect the future confidence of coach and player.

DRESS

Dress properly for the weather. For the game, wear the uniform selected by your local board. If dress is optional, wear neatly pressed gray slacks and a laundered gray or white and black-striped shirt.

Take pains with your footwear. "An official is no better than his feet." You may use a regular shoe with rubber soles and heels or, if you prefer, the black full-sized type. Proper fit is vital. A shoe that is too tight or too large will blister your feet. A good pair of laundered woolen socks will absorb the perspiration.

Carry your footwear in a separate little bag so that it will not soil the other wearing apparel. Have a sweater handy to wear before the game, between the halves and after the game, until you return to the dressing room.

If it is customary for the official to wear a bow tie, do so. The author prefers an open collar and no tie as an aid to easy breathing. An extra pair of shoe laces and an extra whistle should always be carried in the bag.

THE WHISTLE

The whistle may be carried in the hand or laced around the neck. The carried whistle hinders ball-handling and may occasionally be dropped. Hence, the other method is recommended. The whistle should be laced around the neck with sufficient anchorage to prevent it from twisting to the rear.

Whichever method you adopt, learn to use the whistle in split-second time. Carry an extra whistle on the person. The rubber-composition type is safest for the protection of the teeth. If the metal type is used, rubber bands should be wrapped around its mouth.

SPLIT VISION

The eyes can see long distances, but to get a clearer view of the action and to be ready to handle the ball when necessary, you must keep on top of the play. A chauffeur watches the light, the pedestrian, the police officer, and another car, at the same time. Borrow this split-vision motif in your officiating. Watch the ball and the relative positions of players at the same time; shooting quick side glances, when necessary, to take in every player. The slightest turn of the head will locate another area or field of vision.

Your position, stance, observation post, and working area, are all determined by the visual view necessary. Face, swerve, glide, stop, or run, according to the exigency of the situation. The experienced arbiter keeps up with the play, catches the entire picture, and stays clear of all players.

The center-line rule has made it easier to officiate. It gives you less area to cover or check once the offense has brought the ball to the front court.

Take care not to abuse your eyes. Get sufficient sleep and rest and avoid eye strain of any sort, especially reading in poor light or in moving vehicles. Periodic examinations will help safeguard your vision.

FOODS

Avoid foods that disagree with you, especially fatty, fried, spicy, greasy, or rich foods. Eat a varied diet including meats, milk, greens, cereals, and fruits.

Eat lightly at least two hours before game time. After the game, when the body has had time to relax and cool off, a light snack may replenish your energy. Never drink liquor before a game. There is no surer way of losing the respect of the players. After a game, moderate drinkers may find relaxation in a glass of ale or beer.

CARE OF THE FEET

The preliminary training period will satisfactorily condition the feet for the abuse they will be called upon to take. The first few games will finish the toughening process.

To avoid athlete's foot, do not walk barefoot in the dressing room; wear locker-room slippers or wooden shower sandals. The wooden shoes may be kept in a rubber bathing bag.

SHOWER

Always carry your own towel in case the school fails to furnish one. Take a warm shower, gradually turning it to cool. Dry well after the shower and dress. Do not sit around in the nude, discussing the game. Do not leave until the body is cooled and relaxed. If you must catch a train, make arrangements for taxi service beforehand. Keep warmly dressed. Standing around while waiting for transportation invites a cold.

On the train, which is usually too cold or too hot, adjust your clothing accordingly. If you must take a seat next to a window, use your sweater or coat to weather strip the cracks.

You must take these precautions because of your exposure to colds. Outside of the usual cold germ passed from person to person by sneezing, coughing, or water glass, etc., you will come in contact with excessively cold, excessively stuffy, or excessively dry dressing rooms, concrete floors, and rapid changes from hot to cold or dry to wet weather. Avoid chills, wet feet, and drafts. These predispose to colds. Some people are lucky and have a natural resistance to colds; others are highly susceptible. If you cannot rid yourself of a cold within the usual four-day period, see a doctor. Often the colds are due to obstructions in the nose, diseased tonsils adenoids, or sinus conditions that may lower the resistance.

SLEEP

Sleep is the great restorer. When going to bed, relax both mind and body. Forget the tribulations of the day. You need a sound sleep to restore your energy and to prepare for the rigors of the next day.

On long train rides, get in the habit of taking "cat naps." On overnight trips, don't try to save money by sleeping in a chair. Get a pullman berth, if possible. Although you may not sleep well on a train, a berth will always afford more relaxation than a seat.

WORRY

Do not fret. Accept full measure of the responsibility. Do not seek comfort in alcohol. Too many officials worry themselves sick over important games. The veteran takes these contests in stride. He knows the close games are usually easier to handle. Since fouls are too damaging, the players are more cautious.

You will just have to talk yourself out of thinking any game is too tough. New confidence will be gained with every game you work. Facing situations from which one tries to escape builds an immunity to worry.

COURAGE

Courage has been defined as the "quality of mind which shows itself in facing danger without fear." Anybody can look good in a one-sided game. It's how you react under pressure that counts. The nip-and-tuck game, the grudge or traditional game, and the championship game are the real testing grounds for courage.

Call everything you see; instantly, confidently and courageously. Any hesitation is a confession of weakness that the players will be quick to seize upon. Organic fortitude must be built like character or personality. If you have any weaknesses, face them squarely. Work on them constantly. "If you have the courage to face your weaknesses, you will become aware of your strength."

Chapter 2

RATINGS, GAME RELATIONSHIPS, ETHICS

MANY DIFFICULTIES ARISE when one side dictates the choice of official. Expecting an unfair deal, the visitors often arrive with a chip on their shoulders. Their attitude toward the official is bad from the start.

An officials' bureau will insure impartial officiating. This may be worked through the coaches association or through the executive office of the district league. The coaches may rate all the district officials and appoint a commissioner or board to make the assignments. Every visiting team may be given a list of available officials in advance, and thus may check with their opponents when the contract is signed.

Many associations, conferences, and boards rate the officials and, as a check, have the coaches file a report after every game. Frequently, there is a decided discrepancy between the winning coach's estimate of the official and that of the losing coach. Although most coaches venture their honest opinion, there are men who will use the official as an alibi for defeat.

Associate Commissioners Dave Walsh and Ellwood Geiges of the Collegiate Basketball Officials Bureau are very capable men who are doing a good job of reporting on officials, correcting their mistakes, and improving their performances.

Their ratings, coupled with the coaches' reports, are recorded by the Director of the Eastern Intercollegiate Association, Asa Bushnell, who sums up his findings and makes assignments accordingly. The point system is: 5—excellent, 4—above average, 3—average, 2—below average, 1—inferior.

RELATIONSHIP WITH COACH

Once the officials are approved, the coaches should let them work unmolested. Officials are human and thus fallible. But, while coaches and players can make mistakes, the official apparently cannot. One bad night and everybody is ready to ostracize him. It is not unusual for a coach to switch officials at the last minute, or to take a man out of a game. Often a young coach will blackball an official. Despite the fact the official may have been giving excellent service for years, the coach's colleagues will often follow his lead.

Coaches must be in the wrong when a man they reject is used by an overwhelming majority of other coaches. There is no reason why coaches and officials should not get together more often and make an attempt to understand each other's problems.

The irate coach who incites his team and the spectators by bobbing up and down on the bench, or tries to intimidate the official by other actions, is no credit to his profession. No referee minds an occasional outburst by the coach, but he does mind the chronic "beefer." Since the coaches have agreed upon the officials, they must have the confidence in him to give him free rein. Trying to sway the official or "ride" him is unsportsmanlike conduct.

Assuming you are the official: Adopt a polite but firm attitude toward the coach. Make him feel that you are the sole boss of the game, but that you are always ready to listen to anything he has to say. By your precise, sure actions, show that you will brook no nonsense. Do not fraternize with either coach. It is poor psychology. The opposing coach and players may feel you're against them.

RELATIONSHIP WITH PLAYERS

Adopt a friendly attitude toward the players. It isn't necessary to assert authority too strongly. Putting fear into the boys hinders their playing and antagonizes them.

The players will usually be willing to co-operate with you. Of course, now and then a boy will act up, especially on his fourth or disqualifying foul. But if he doesn't get abusive, do not penalize him. You must distinguish between ill temper directed at you, which must be called, and actions which indicate the player is just annoyed at himself.

If this burst of temperament is intended to arouse the sympathy of the crowd or the coach, quickly call a technical foul. The situation has its parallel in baseball, where the batter turns and tongue-lashes the umpire for calling a third strike. If the player is popular, the spectators will invariably side with him.

RELATIONSHIP WITH SPECTATORS

Again courage is a prime asset. Turn a deaf ear to any "riding" by the spectators. Poise is necessary. Show the spectators you are not easily swayed or rattled, but have the courage of your convictions. Even the so-called "wolves" who came to have a good time at your expense, will respect you.

Sometimes an outcry will be raised in one section of the audience, perhaps because they failed to see the last finger-touch that caused a ball to go out of bounds. In a fine play of this kind, always *emphasize* your decision by *demonstrating* what happened and pointing to the player who caused the out.

NOISY CROWD

In a nip-and-tuck affair, pandemonium may break loose. Cowbells, horns and other noisemakers may drown out the whistle. If a player fails to hear the whistle, keep tooting loud, successive, short blasts, and chase the play to stop it.

Referee Pat Kennedy, one of the greatest officials in the game, had this happen in the national championship college game of 1943, when the Wyoming team failed to hear the whistle for a time-out called by St. Johns on an out-of-bound ball. The capable Kennedy ran down the entire floor, whistling, but a goal was scored by Wyoming before he could stop the play. This would have been the winning goal, had it not been declared void. Fortunately, the Wyoming coach heard the official's frantic blasts. The game went into overtime. A game that close will always cause enough bedlam to drown out the whistle. It may help to appeal to the crowd to stop blowing horns or ringing bells when the ball is in play.

UNSCRUPULOUS OFFICIALS

No matter how many games you officiate for a certain team, never give them an "edge." Let the home team respect you for your skill and courage, not for your favors. The "homer" type of official is no credit to his profession. Keep your courage high and your integrity above reproach.

UNIFORMITY

Intersectional matches were once a constant source of trouble and dispute. Provincial interpretation of the rules sowed many disagreements. Officials were finicky on some calls and too liberal on others; one section favored the offense, another the defense, and so on.

It is not an easy matter to balance a game through the rules. A game must afford equal opportunities for the offense and defense to show their speed, guile and power. In the case of basketball, the misunderstandings among coaches, players, and officials were not the fault of the rules, but of the different interpretations given them in various milieus.

A few years ago, the word "block" would have caused an all-night discussion at any meeting of basketballers. Now the screening rule has been framed to the satisfaction of all, and the "block" is no longer a controversial subject. We have progressed rapidly because every section conceded a bit. The sectional and national meetings of coaches, officials, and writers also helped settle disputes and promote uniformity in the interpretation of the rules.

At the clinical demonstrations throughout the country, coaches, officials, and players were able to air their views and know what decisions could be expected in various play situations. At present, we have more intersectional matches than ever, with record attendance.

Much can be gained by frequent coach-official meetings in which both parties can study each other's problems, iron out any differences, and arrive at definite policies and objectives.

Chapter 3

PRINCIPLES AND TIME ELEMENTS

ALTHOUGH BASKETBALL IS essentially a non-contact game, personal contact cannot be entirely avoided. When ten players are moving rapidly in limited areas, contact is bound to occur. Their chief reasons for fouling include:

1. Lack of speed or inability to stay with faster opponents.
2. Lack of co-ordination and skill.
3. Height handicaps, where smaller players, unable to gain possession of the ball resort to fouling.
4. Inability to relax in split-second time or uncontrolled speed and aggressiveness.
5. Faulty screening.
6. Poor timing and judgment.
7. Fatigue.
8. Intentional fouling to prevent sure goals.
9. Intentional fouling by the losers when the opponents use stalling tactics.
10. Over-anxiousness.

Skillful players foul less than awkward ones. It is also true that more fouls are committed in a grudge or traditional game than in an ordinary contest. You must accept these fouls as part of the game and trust they will not interfere too much with the continuity of play.

Constant whistle blowing does not necessarily decrease the number of fouls. The character of the game determines that. The game must be taken in hand from the very beginning. The players must know that you mean business.

TYPES OF FOULS

Experience will teach you what fouls are involved in various situations.

1. If the offense uses screening and weaving tactics, be alert for illegal screening and blocking.

2. If a fast break is used, watch for traveling violations; it is more difficult to control the ball at high speed than it is in slower, deliberate maneuvers.

3. If the defense uses a zone, screening is less likely but watch for guarding from the rear and blocking out by guards on rebounds.

4. If the pivot or double post is used, be alert for rear and lateral illegal screening and "jockeying" for position by the posts.

5. If stalling tactics are used, watch for intentional fouling by the defense.

WHISTLE BLOWING

Blowing your whistle prematurely in anticipation of fouls or violations is a bad habit. It is just as bad as blowing your whistle too late. Perfect timing is essential. At the same time, do not kill the game by tooting a melody throughout. The spirit of the rules must be kept in mind and common sense applied lest the game degenerate into a foul-shooting contest. Rules are necessary, but must be tempered with sound judgment.

If you cannot distinguish between meaningless nudges that do no harm and the slightest push that does damage, you will never become a good official. Learn to recognize favorable and unfavorable positions of the players when contact occurs. Unavoidable contacts from favorable positions are not fouls. Unfortunately there are officials who are not happy, and do not feel they have earned their fees, unless they call forty or fifty fouls a game.

It is a coach's responsibility to control his team when it starts committing too many fouls. This happens occasionally in grudge or traditional games. If the players want to fight instead of play, all the whistles in the world won't prevent them from fouling.

The Block: It is the coach's prerogative to teach forward, lateral or rear screening; these are fine arts. But if the players cannot execute these plays without blocking—that is, illegal screening, then other methods of attack should be encouraged.

Consistency: The lax official who sometimes lets the players fight it out, or becomes sympathetic and stops calling fouls on the losing team in a one-sided contest, will lose control of the game. Consistency is necessary. You are not rated on the number of fouls you call but strictly on the judgment you use.

The most capable officials under any working system pick up the knack of being in the right places at the right times. The "tricks of the trade," the knowledge of the techniques of the game, the anticipation of the direction of play, and the readiness for types of fouls involved in various situations, come with experience.

TIME ELEMENTS

The three-second foul-lane, ten-second center-line, and five-second throw-in rules are essential parts of the game. You must count to yourself whenever the situation arises; at the same time observing any other infractions. The secret count is stopped when play indicates it is no longer necessary.

The criticism directed at many officials is that they count too fast. The back-to-front-court ten-second rule is seldom violated because ten seconds are ample to bring the ball to the front court. However, if you notice a pressing defense in the back court, pick up the count immediately, calling the seconds from six to ten *out loud.*

In the five-second count on out-of-bound throw-ins, statistics show that there is very little delay, and that the thrower usually gets the pass away in less than four seconds.

The most abused calculation is the three-second count in the foul lane from the end line to the foul line. The rule states "The offensive must not be timed when the ball is dead, is in the air, or on a try for a goal, or while it is rebounding from the backboard. Allowance must also be made for a player, who having been in the restricted area for less than three seconds, dribbles in to shoot for a goal."

Many officials take up the count regardless of these exceptions. The author suggests that officials practice accuracy in timing by counting one-thousand-and-one, one-thousand-and-two, etc., for each second. Practice this method of counting at home using a stop watch. Have someone test your accuracy until you are as nearly perfect as can be expected.

Scorers and timers must be trained for their duties as table officials before the season starts. Many a game can be ruined by the inefficiency of these officials. Referees should assist whenever the home management or coach desires information as to proper timing and scoring or a better understanding of the code or signals.

Chapter 4

DUTIES OF THE SINGLE OFFICIAL

NO MATTER HOW GIFTED an official you may be, it is humanly impossible for you to cover the court as adequately as two men. Unfortunately, many schools cannot afford two officials. But, while they hire only one, they still insist on a perfectly administered game. As a solo official, your lot is not a happy one. To do a good job, you must devise a system that will keep you on top of the action, thus reducing your margin of error.

Since the entire court must be covered, speed is essential. Wherever and whenever ball-handling is required or a foul or violation called, be a "johnny-on-the-spot." After a call, immediately face the table officials, signal properly, etc., so that the decision is clear to everybody. Cross the court only when necessary, and remain on that side until forced to cross again.

WORKING AREA OF THE SINGLE OFFICIAL

Your working area should be inside the court, about four or five feet from the side line. Move parallel to the side lines but go no farther than either foul line.

When the offense is controlling the ball in the front court, take your stance at the observation post. This post is opposite the foul line, about four or five feet inside the side line. From this spot, glide in the direction of the ball.

If the defense is pressing back court or around the middle, drop back for a better view. Do *not* go to the end line, as the leading official does in the double-referee system. An interception

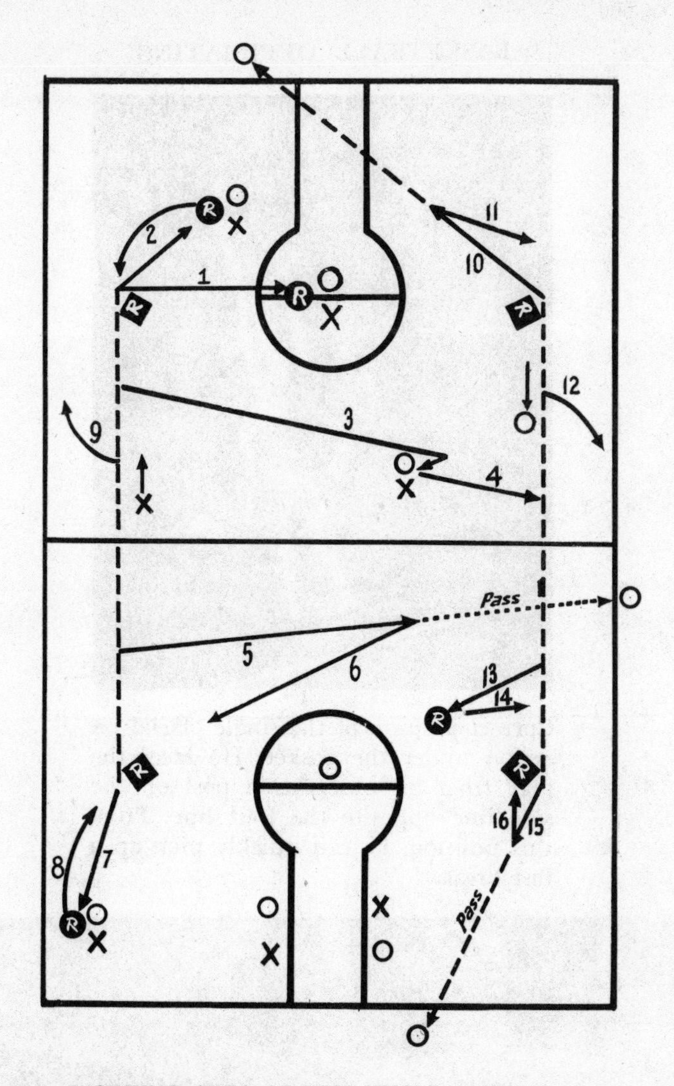

WORKING AREA OF THE SINGLE OFFICIAL

1. Handling a jump ball in the foul lane
2. Clearing and gliding back to observation post while facing play
3. Crossing court for a jump ball
4. Clearing to nearer side and breaking to whatever side play indicates
5. Running in, and using "pitch" method for a throw-in
6. Fading back to same side
7. Handling a jump ball in right corner
8. Clearing and getting back
9. Clearing to side line to avoid a player
10. "Pitch" method to end line for a throw-in
11. Clearing after pitch
12. Clearing to nearer side line to avoid ball
13. Taking charge of the foul shot
14. Clearing to side after shot, facing play
15. "Pitch" to end line for a throw-in
16. Clearing back to the observation post

Correct position of the single official on action under the basket. He faces the play from his observation post on the side line opposite the foul line. From this position, he can quickly pick up a fast break.

Incorrect position of the single official—he is too deep. Because his view is obscured by the players' bodies, he cannot see the knee block on the dribbler. A fast break will catch him flat-footed.

or change in possession, accompanied by a fast break, will leave you far behind the play.

From the observation post, you get a diagonal panorama of the action. You are ready for anything. With experience, you will soon learn not to over-run or get left behind.

It is essential to know the mechanics of deliberate offenses, weaving or figure-eight tactics, criss-crossing, screening, pivot plays, fast breaks, and man-to-man, zone and other defenses. Without a working knowledge of these techniques, you will tend to concentrate on the ball and miss the offenders. A thorough understanding will also enable you to pace yourself properly, so that you can jog, clear, glide, stop, or speed ahead as the situations demand.

CLEARANCE

In the double-referee system, there is little chance of interference, since the officials' working area is on the outside of the court. In the one-man game, however, where you work on the inside, interference is a distinct possibility. Many situations demand your clearing or crossing the court.

When a player or pass is headed toward you, clear to the nearer side line. If it is impossible to clear without interference, dodge or step aside until you find room to clear. This situation may be minimized by constant alertness. Suggestions on clearance on the throw-ins and the toss may be found in those chapters.

STANCE TAKEN AT THE OBSERVATION POST

If the play indicates continuity by the offense, take a comfortable stance in the observation post. Your stance should resemble that of the football halfback.

The legs are about two feet apart with the weight equally distributed, knees slightly bent, trunk inclined forward with a slight bend at the hips, hands resting on knees or thighs, and head erect. The eyes follow the play with effective split vision to focus the entire picture.

A good, comfortable stance with which to observe play in the front court. Hands are on knees and body is turned toward the mass of players.

The crouch position when play is centered in the corner. The official has edged toward the side line for a close-quarters view of the action.

Sway from side to side with the play by shifting your weight toward the direction desired and slightly straightening the knee on the opposite side. This is necessary at times to get an unobstructed view.

You must be ready to push off either foot instantly for a glide or a fast break. Never turn your back to the play when clearing to the sides or reversing your field. The glide is a boxing step.

This picture was taken before working areas were clearly defined. That's why the arbiters are not sandwiching the play. Under the present system, the official in the background would be in his observation post under the basket.

The trailing official (foreground) is too far down the sideline. He will never be able to get ahead of or keep up with a fast break. He should be back opposite the foul line.

The leading official reaping the benefit of good position play. Despite the fact that an attacker has broken completely into the clear, the official has been able to get ahead of the play.

The trailing official correctly advancing with the play. His partner (not seen here) is moving ahead of the play along the opposite side line.

Chapter 5

THE DOUBLE-OFFICIAL SYSTEM

THE DOUBLE-OFFICIAL SYSTEM is the most efficient now in use. It has been perfected through trial and error in every section of the country. When properly employed, it does away with guess-work from "center field" and "standing on a dime." Neither does it require the arbiters to run themselves ragged; it covers all exigencies.

The officials work diagonally, keeping in mind that they must sandwich the play between them. The mechanics of the double-

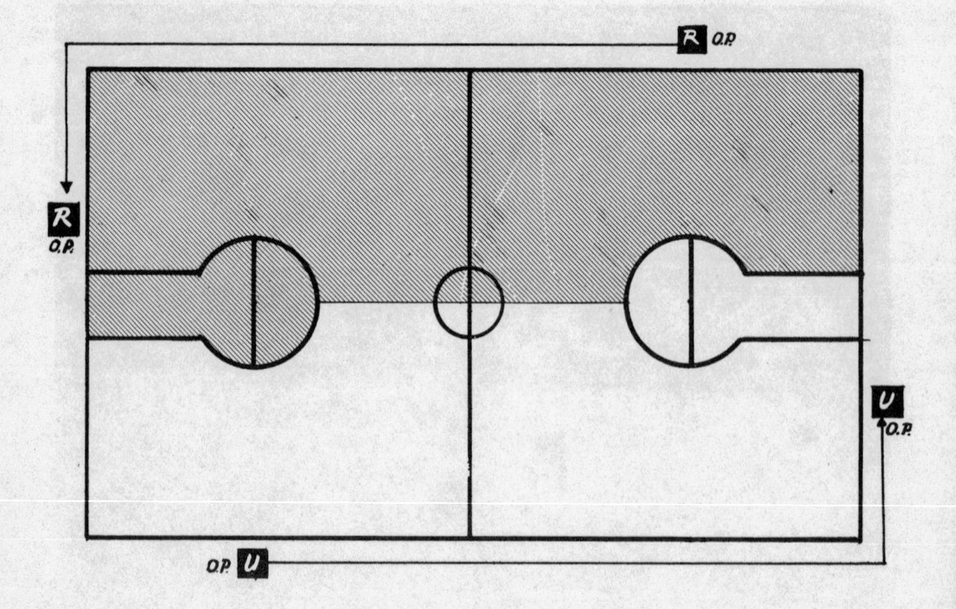

DIAGRAM 1, Working Areas

official system are outlined in the accompanying diagram. The diagrams chart the relative positioning and the shuttling actions in the common game situations.

The key is simple: R connotes the Referee; U, the Umpire; and O. P., Observation Post.

WORKING AREAS

In Diagram 1, on page 24, the shaded area is the Referee's chief responsibility.

The non-shaded area is the Umpire's chief responsibility.

Both officials' work on the outside, about two feet from the side lines and end lines, and move parallel to these lines.

The man on each end covers the entire end line for out-of-bounds balls.

Both officials go deep to their right; that is, to the outside of the end line slightly right of the basket. These spots are shown by the squares about two feet from the end line. These are the observation posts, or vantage grounds from which the officials may observe the action. From these posts their arc of vision will take in the areas where most fouls are committed.

From underneath the basket, both officials go left as far as the foul line extended to the side line.

Each official stays in his own half court.

The official takes charge of the foul-lane plays (commonly called the keyhole) and the three-second rule on his right only.

The trailing man covers the ten-second rule, back to the front court.

In this system one official will always be ahead of the play.

CENTER TOSS

In Diagram 2, on page 26, the referee faces the table officials; that is, the scorers and timers. He stands about arm's distance away from the jumpers, to see that they are in proper position.

The umpire stands on the outside slightly to the right of the jumpers, opposite the referee.

Both officials break after play is indicated. The arrows show the directions in which they may move.

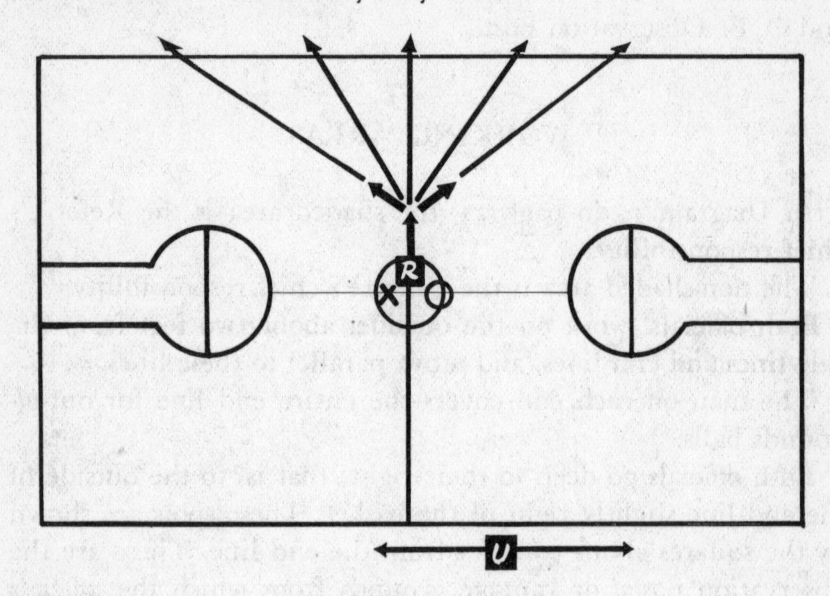

DIAGRAM 2, Center Toss

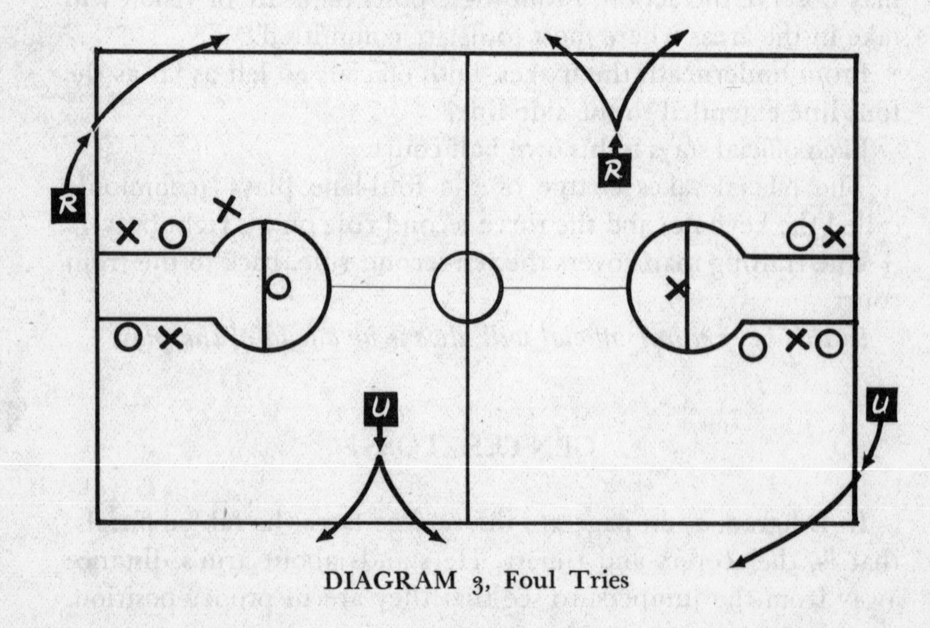

DIAGRAM 3, Foul Tries

FOUL TRIES

(See Diagram 3, page 26.)

During a foul try, the trailing official takes charge of the shot, while the leading official takes his position deep underneath, as he would on an offensive advance to the basket on his right. The arrows show the directions in which the officials may break after play is indicated.

The trailer should stand at least six feet to the left and behind the foul circle. This gives him ample room and time to clear to the outside after the shot. It is important that both men glide until it is safe to run with the play.

After a field goal or a foul shot is made, it isn't necessary to handle the ball. The opponents must step outside the end line to take possession.

JUMP BALLS IN FOUL LANES

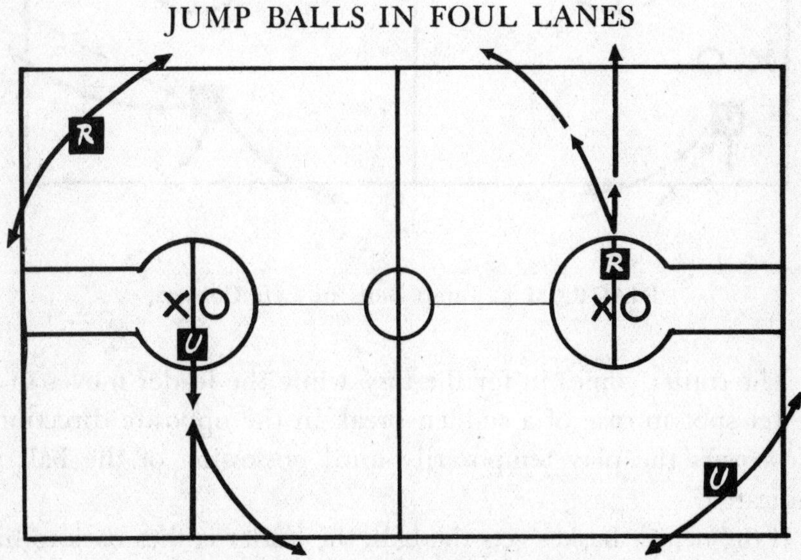

DIAGRAM 4, Jump Balls in Foul Lanes.

The trailer takes charge of the jumps in the lanes. The leader takes a position near the corner that will diagonally face the play and sandwich it.

Arrows show the directions in which they may break after the play is indicated, and get to their best working territories.

If the nearer basket obtains possession after the toss, the leader quickly gets underneath and the trailer clears to the nearer side line. They will then be at their respective observation posts.

JUMP BALLS IN LEFT CORNERS

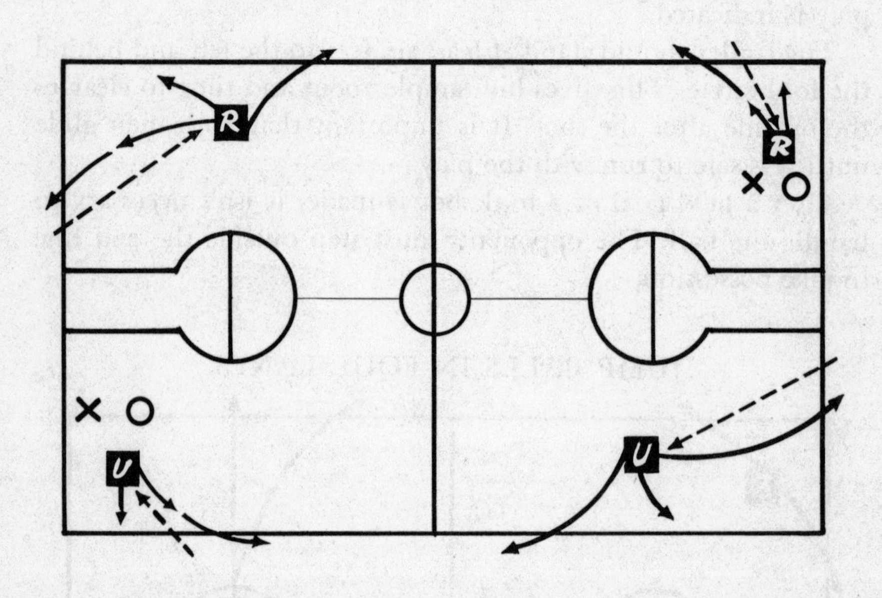

DIAGRAM 5, Jump Balls in Left Corners

The trailer comes in for the toss, while the leader moves to a better spot in case of a sudden break in the opposite direction. He covers the play temporarily until possession of the ball is indicated.

If the nearer basket gets the ball, the leader rushes back to his observation post behind the end line, while the trailer glides back to his post at the foul line extended (side line).

Dotted arrows show the officials leaving their observation posts.

Chapter 6

HANDLING GAME SITUATIONS

SCREENING

NEVER ANTICIPATE CONTACT. In an illegal screen play, for example, the victim may back away or clear. An over-anxious official, anticipating the block, may blow his whistle, only to find no contact has occurred. If you make this mistake, return the ball to the offense at the nearest out-of-bounds spot.

FAST TAKE-OUTS

In cross-court maneuvers, a speedy offensive player may cut across court for a lateral screen. He may time his stop so that the guard has no chance to clear. The screener's teammate, whose guard is trapped, breaks across the court a split-second before the screener stops. This break in the opposite direction runs the guard into the screener.

The rule places the responsibility on the moving offensive screener. On plays of this type, you must decide the following:

1. Did the screener allow at least three-feet clearance after he stopped? If he did, the play is legal.

2. Did the screener stop less than three feet behind the guard? Was he moving when contact was established? In either case, the foul is on the screener.

3. Did the guard, who was given the prescribed leeway and time to clear, deliberately run into the screener? This is a foul on the guard.

Legal screen play: As the out-of-bounds man holds up the ball, a teammate sneaks up behind the guard and stops about five feet behind him. The thrower tosses the ball to another teammate (not in picture) and cuts sharply off the stationary screen, running his man into him. The contact is legal, as the screener has given the guard the prescribed three-feet leeway.

Illegal screen play: This time the screener stops directly behind the guard, so that the latter has no chance of avoiding contact. Hence, the ensuing contact is a foul on the screener.

Left: Fouls in Bucket. Ball-handler pinches guard's arms with his upper arms to make it appear as though the guard is holding.

Right: The guard keeps his body clear, but ties up the ball-handler by pinching his upper arms with his own (guard's) arms.

Screening Post: Watch the post or bucket player on rear screens. See that he gives the guard at least three-feet leeway in his screening operation. If he does, it is a legal play and the contact is overlooked. Don't be fooled by a guard who anticipates the screen and deliberately walks into it to draw a foul. The foul is on the guard.

If the guard does not see the screener and backs into him, do not call a foul on him (guard). However, call a foul on any legally screened guard who deliberately roughs the screener. Also see that the guard, after being legally screened, does not push the screener.

A more subtle fouler is the offensive player who grazes the guard's shoulder just enough to retard his progress or upset his stride. The trick is usually pulled during fast-weaving or figure-eight tactics, where it may go unnoticed.

THE "BUCKET" (PIVOT OR POST)

The offensive bucket player who backs into his guard is fouling. If the guard has taken his position behind the bucket legally, the bucket must avoid contact.

The bucket cannot raise his arms sideways to prevent the guard from cutting around to intercept a pass. If contact is caused by the bucket's arms, charge him with a blocking foul.

Another common trick in the bucket is intentionally bending the trunk forward to hip the guard out of position. Some bucket players have a trick of wheeling around suddenly to push the guard into an unfavorable position. This is a charging foul.

A foul is also committed when the bucket, in turning with the ball for a one-handed shot, elbows the guard. This stunt is often missed by officials who watch the shooting arm only. The burden is still on the ball-handler. He must make an attempt to circumvent the guard, even though his back is turned to the guard.

The bucket may avoid contact by stepping forward in the clear, then turning and shooting; or make sure he wheels to the sides with sufficient clearance.

Blocking: Very often, the bucket will suddenly step out to

Foul by the pivot-post shooter for elbowing. This stunt is often missed by officials who watch the shooting arm only.

block (pick-off) a teammate's opponent who has honestly crossed the bucket's path in chasing his man. The fact that the bucket has the ball and is permitted to pivot, doesn't give him the right to block out an oncoming opponent. He must give the chasing guard sufficient time to avoid contact.

When guards are run into the bucket, make sure the bucket has given the necessary three-feet leeway and hasn't walked in to cause the contact.

When play is fast, you must use peripheral vision to observe closely the relative positioning and distances between players. With experience, you'll sense which player is assuming the role

Fouls in Bucket. The ball-handler is backing up; that is, stepping back and hipping his man away from the ball.

Foul is by the defensive man (dark shirt) for waving his hand in front of the bucket's eyes to obstruct his vision.

Drawing a Foul. The ball-handler has pivoted and is about to lay up the ball with a two-hand underhand release. Any attempt by the guard to block the shot will look like hacking.

Kneeing the Bucket. While feigning an honest attempt at the ball with his hands, the guard presses his knee into the hollow behind the ball-handler's knee joint.

Illegal turn-around. The pivot waits for his teammate to cut by; as latter's guard follows up, the ball-handler pivots to cut him off. Foul is on the ball-handler, unless he has pivoted in time to permit the guard to avoid him.

of bucket or post. Running guards into posts is clever maneuvering and legal, provided the three-foot rule is observed.

See that the bucket does not stray over the end line purposely, then suddenly dash back on the court to a strategic spot. This is a technical foul for unsportsmanlike conduct.

After receiving the ball, the bucket may maneuver the guard's outstretched arms under his and clutch them with his own upper arms. The fact that the bucket has the ball makes it appear as though the guard is holding. The foul is on the bucket. Watch for fouls by buckets who jockey for position before ball arrives.

Defensive Fouls: Watch the guard for body-pushing. Don't be fooled if he raises his arms sideways to show his innocence. If the bucket has legally taken his position, and is being pushed by the guard, it is a foul on the guard.

The guard may "feel out" his opponent by resting his hand or hands on the offensive player. This is a foul. Call it immediately. Don't wait until the guard exerts pressure to hold off his opponent. Hand resters invariably cause trouble, as their opponents usually resort to slapping or elbowing to rid themselves of this annoyance.

Watch the guard who intentionally steps on the bucket's feet, feigning interception of a pass. Or who holds the bucket's belt to prevent him from jumping or following up a shot. The leading official is in the best position to catch these offenders. Sometimes the guard will place one knee under the bucket's knee and with slight body or arm pressure and knee bend, trip the bucket. This, of course, is a foul.

A technical foul for unsportsmanlike conduct should be called on the guard who waves his hand in front of the bucket's eyes to obstruct his view.

DRIBBLING

Study the dribbling rules carefully. Traveling is not difficult to detect if you observe the two-count rhythm that is permitted a player after completing a dribble or after receiving the ball while moving. The chief factor to determine is whether or not the ball has rested. With the exception of one air dribble, if the

Fouling the dribbler. The dribbler, Hank Luisetti, has circumvented his man and is going in for the lay up. The guard is distinctly in an unfavorable position. To break up the play, he is hitting Luisetti with his body and arm.

The foul here is by the dribbler. He is forcing his way through with his shoulder and hip. If the dribbler hadn't charged, the guard's extended arm might have provoked a foul.

ball, after contacting the floor, comes to rest in one or both hands, or is touched with both hands, the dribble is completed.

Watch the position of the feet at the end of a dribble. If the player stops in a side-stride position, either foot may be used as the pivot foot. If he stops with one foot forward, the rear foot is considered the pivot foot.

It is no violation to start dribbling after slapping the ball out of an opponent's hands and catching it off the bounce. The player may use the slap as the start of his dribble or catch the ball after the slap, and then start his dribble. Some officials err in counting the bounce caused by the slap before control was gained.

Steps: A player may take as many steps between bounces as he desires, as long as the ball is not resting. Players often push the ball ahead on the last bounce, run up to meet it, catch it, then shoot or pass. This is legal though it may seem the player is traveling.

Cupping: Cupping the ball is considered resting it. This is done occasionally by a player who, while dribbling, turns his palm upward to improve his control of the ball. The dribble ceases as soon as the player cups the ball. If he continues to dribble after cupping (resting) the ball, it is a violation.

Step and Leap After Dribble: If the player attempts a lay-up shot after a dribble, he is permitted a step and leap after the ball has come to rest in one or both hands. Thus he may pass or shoot while in the air before the rear foot or both feet retouch the floor. Many officials wrongly call a violation on this play, especially on tall players, who appear to be traveling when they take a long step and lay-out.

Shot from Pivot: The pivot is permitted before or after the dribble. You must observe the stationary or so-called pivot foot. If it is raised, the ball must be released before that foot retouches the floor.

When the pivoter turns to take his shot, he is permitted the same step and leap, provided the step is taken with the movable, (not the pivot) foot.

If the player received the ball while standing still, or came to

Two common forms of "hands" fouls. Above, the black-shirted player in the foreground is feeling out his man to make certain he doesn't go around him. Below, the white-shirted rebounder nearest the camera is using his left arm to push the retriever. This foul should be caught by the trailing official, as the leading official on the end line is in poor position to see it.

a legal stop while holding the ball, he may lift the pivot foot or turn and jump when he shoots or passes, but the ball must leave his hands before one or both feet again touch the floor.

All this may sound complicated, but as an official you must quickly "spot" the foot being used as the pivot.

Toddling: Taking alternate short steps in place with the ball resting in hand or hands, is a violation.

Co-ordination: Players who lack co-ordination and a sense of timing in taking off for a lay-up shot, will give you the most trouble. These players invariably rest the ball too soon, then proceed to travel in order to get closer to the basket. In most cases the violator is out in the open where the violation is simple to detect.

Avoiding Contact: You must watch the relative positioning of the dribbler and the guard in front of him. The dribbler must attempt to go around the guard to avoid contact. Look for favorable and unfavorable positions of both players. If the dribbler goes around, the guard must make his move for the ball. If the guard deliberately steps into the dribbler's path and contact occurs, the foul is on the guard.

On the other hand, if the guard maintained his position legally and the dribbler charged into him, the foul is on the dribbler.

If the guard, in raising his arms to block the dribbler's path, causes contact, it is a foul.

Do not be mislead by the guard who feigns an honest attempt at the ball but charges the dribbler with his body. At the same time, see that the dribbler does not use his free elbow or shoulder to ward off the guard.

Sudden Stop: Do not penalize a closely trailing guard who contacts the dribbler after a sudden stop by the latter. It is the dribbler's privilege to stop short or pull up at any time. You must decide whether or not the guard was able to avoid the contact. If the guard had sufficient time and room to avoid contact and did not, call a charging foul on him.

Contact of this kind often occurs, with one or both players falling to the floor. If you feel the contact was accidental and unavoidable, do not stop the play. If both players have their hands on the ball, a held ball is in order. If the dribbler was not content to stop short, but intentionally hipped the guard even for protection, then charge the dribbler with a personal foul. Never should a closely trailing guard be charged for contact caused by a dribbler's sudden stop.

Hazards: On many high school courts, walls, bleacher seats, or other hazards congest the area under the baskets. Here again you must decide whether or not there is charging from the rear by the guard or whether the contact was caused by an offensive player who stopped short for fear of hitting the walls, etc.

Fumbles: Fumbles are not considered dribbles. However, you must not confuse a fumble with a dropped ball provoked by close guarding. In the latter case, determine whether or not a violation has been committed according to the dribble rule.

Second Guess: Never second guess. Some coaches advocate the ignoring of fouls that do not bother a dribbler going in for a sure basket. These coaches, however, invariably object when the sure basket is missed.

The coach scored against also wonders why the foul was not called. When officials ignore these fouls, the guards will become exceptionally rough to make sure the foul is not overlooked. This is dangerous. Call the foul immediately.

Accidental Foul: A trailing guard who steps on the heel of a dribbler ahead of him, tripping the latter, should be charged with a foul even though the trip was accidental. The guard must be considered as having been in an unfavorable position.

REBOUNDS

Watch the territory underneath the basket and instantly decide the players' rights to positions. Do not concentrate on the flight of the ball but observe closely the movements of players, especially when the ball is on its downward path.

Riding: Watch the player who illegally gains possession of the ball by climbing or "riding" the back of an opponent. This is a charging foul.

Wedge: Penalize defensive players who form a wedge in the

In maneuvering for favorable positions on rebounds, the players are frequently guilty of excessive roughness. One of the more common fouls is blocking or "holding out," which may be observed in the foreground of the top picture and under the basket in the bottom picture.

paths of offensive retrievers, and block out by stepping back and causing contact, or raise their arms sideways to cause contact.

Pushing: Penalize the offensive player who pushes or charges a guard who legally attained a favorable position.

Blocking: Penalize the guard who deliberately steps into the path of an oncoming offensive player to block him out.

Spread Eagle: Penalize the man who goes up in spread-eagle fashion and kicks his opponent. The jumper is taking more room than he needs. The same applies to the jumper who jackknifes and hits his opponent with his hips.

No Jump: Do not call a jump when you see several players aggresively leaping for the ball. This is unfair to the players.

Unavoidable Falls: Often two opponents leap for the ball in an honest attempt to gain possession. The slightest nudge may cause a fall. Do not be swayed by the fall of one player and penalize the other. Unavoidable contacts occur often, despite the fact that two opponents are in favorable positions. Sometimes, in deflecting the ball, a player already off-balance may land badly and fall, or attempt to reach beyond his capacity and incline too far forward. Do not base your decision on circumstantial evidence; actually see the foul.

OUT-OF-BOUNDS

You do not have to handle the ball in the attackers' back court. In the front court, however, quickly get the ball and snappily pass it to the man out of bounds. Usually, the thrower commits himself. If no offensive thrower responds, designate the offensive player closest to the out-of-bounds spot. If you are working *alone* and the throw-in is on your side of the court, control the ball properly, pass it to the thrower, and get ahead of the play. Standing too close to the thrower may interfere with the pass.

If the throw-in is on the opposite side of the court, you may do one of three things, depending on the set-up: (1) Come in about half-way across the court, get the ball, immediately pitch it to the thrower, and quickly fade back to the side you left. (2) Pitch to the thrower and cross the court ahead of the play, if the

Wrong position on out-of-bounds play. The official is standing too close to the outside man, cramping his throwing arm and hampering his freedom of movement.

Correct position on outside ball. The official is well removed from the thrower, giving the player complete freedom of movement.

Single official incorrectly handling an end-line throw-in. If play develops to opposite basket, he will be left behind.

Correct method of handling the end-line throw-in. The official uses the pitch method from the side line; leaving him in favorable position for the ensuing play.

set-up indicates you can do so without interference. (3) Pitch to the thrower and cross the court, breaking behind the offensive's safety man, if the latter is not too far back; then work your way ahead.

The relative positioning of the potential receivers and defenders, the readiness of the thrower and the spot along the side-line where the throw is taken, should all be considered in making your decision.

If the throw is to be taken on the side line near either foul line extended, eliminate number two. If the play is out near the middle, you will find number three the safest, as most receivers will either break toward the thrower or toward the basket. The safety man usually fakes an advance and drops back for a pass. If you feel it is necessary to cross, loop the ball slightly to the thrower. This will give you time to gain a few strides toward getting into position.

If time out is called on the out-of-bound, remember the spot of the throw-in. Have both captains acknowledge the ready signal before putting the ball in play on time in.

End Line Throw-Ins: In handling end-line throw-ins, the nearer official in the double-referee system takes charge of the play. The single referee should cut in as much as is necessary to handle the ball, pass it to the thrower and promptly drop back to the nearer side line, gliding to his observation post as soon as possible.

Officials should not pass the ball haphazardly, lob it lazily, or poke it into the thrower's abdomen. They should make a snappy pass toward the thrower's chest.

Controlling the Ball: In front-court situations, control the ball completely before handing or tossing it to the nearest offensive player. Face as many players as possible when announcing your decision and assist by pointing in the direction the ball is to go.

Delaying: If, on an out-of-bound throw-in under the offensive basket, the offensive team delays (within time limits) in getting to set positions, be alert for a screen play. Watch the players, and follow the ball only if it is on your side of the court.

Screening Post: Watch a post player who faces his basket on an

Correct method of following play on an end-line throw-in after a basket. The official is edging along the end line and watching the ball at the same time. Thus, he can see any infraction in the back court or break fast on a long pass.

Incorrect method. The official has turned his head and started up court in anticipation of a long pass or fast break. Any fouling in the back court will thus go unnoticed. An interception will also catch him unprepared.

1
2
3
4
5
6

The toss: *(Starting with picture No. 1 on page 50.)* The official stands arms' length away from jumpers in stride position. The weight is forward, back knee slightly bent and heel raised. The ball is released with an upward wrist snap, arms following through. After toss, the official pushes off forward foot and rocks back on rear heel. He retreats with short, quick, running steps, raising elbows for protection against charging forwards.

out-of-bound throw-in. Teammates may attempt to run their guards into the post. Make sure the post hasn't backed into the guard and violated the three-foot screening rule. The fact that the post has his back turned in contacting the guard, fools many officials.

Face Guarding: Some face guarding is evident on out-of-bound plays, but the rule covers this situation. Some defensive players cleverly shift with their opponents. If, during this shifting by a guard, the attacker makes a legal attempt to go around and the guard steps into his path, causing contact, it is a personal foul on the guard.

Five-Second Count: After an offensive player has received the ball for a front-court throw-in, start your silent five-second count. Do not be misled if the offensive changes players for the throw-in. The count starts from the time the original out-of-bound player received the ball. If a throw has not been made within the time limit, a violation should be called, and the opponents given the ball. These changes occur often when the offense has a set play in mind.

Stalling: Watch for the trick of asking for an official time-out to tie shoe laces. Players will try this when their team has exhausted its time-outs, or to give the trickster's teammates more time to set up an out-of-bound play. Use sensible judgment and notice immediately whether the player's shoe laces have actually become untied.

Delaying the Game: A technical foul should be called immediately on (a) the *defensive* player who tosses the ball to you via sky route, giving him time to get to a more advantageous position. (b) The *offensive* player who uses this stunt for an advantage either in stalling for time or position. (c) The player who intentionally throws to the farther official for some advantage. (d) Rolling the ball slowly to you to delay the game. (e) Delaying a throw-in from out of bounds by stepping outside and touching the ball (defensive player must be back three feet).

No Three Seconds: No count should be started against an offensive player in the three-second foul lane when his teammate has not thrown the ball in from out of bounds. Players must be given their full five seconds for a throw-in. The three-second violation begins when the thrower puts the ball in play.

JUMP BALLS

Dash in for jump balls with all haste possible. If there is an unavoidable delay, call time out immediately.

The idea is to get the ball quickly, designate the jumpers, and stand with your back to the nearer side line. The jumpers may be slow in setting themselves, but you should always be ready for them. Alertness commands respect.

Time taken from the whistle to the toss varies from five to eight seconds. If you're working the game alone, remain on the same side as the toss until you must cross the court. If a held ball occurs just outside the circle, set up the toss in the circle so that the non-jumpers will have a restraining line.

Stance and Clearance: Stand arms' length away from the jumpers. Keep one foot advanced about 12 to 16 inches from the other, with the weight forward. The back knee is slightly bent and the heel raised. The ball is grasped with fingers spread, palms cupped, and elbows slightly bent. It is released with a slight upward snap of the wrists, the arms following through and directing the path of the ball.

After the toss, push off the forward foot and rock back on the rear heel, taking short, quick, running steps backward.

Tossing the ball is an art that is perfected through experience. It must be perfect. If it is too high it will throw the jumpers off their timing. If too low, it may be beaten.

Over-anxiety often causes fouls. To avoid this, steady the jumpers before the toss. A crooked toss may also cause a foul. If you feel the first toss was defective or if neither player tapped it, be man enough to order a re-toss.

One or Two Hand Toss: You may toss the ball with one hand or with two. The two-hand toss is more dependable and is better controlled. Accuracy is essential. Practice the toss so that you will not slant the ball away from the jumpers on your backward step.

Toss higher than the jumpers can leap. Sometimes it is advis-

The toss under actual game conditions. The official has just released the ball and is following through nicely with the arms. The knee of the rear leg is bent and the heel is slightly raised.

Clearing after the toss. Note how the official has rocked backward and raised his elbows for protection against charging forwards. He will now retreat with short, quick, running steps.

able to step momentarily behind the taller jumper or the one most likely to control the tap, then clear out quickly into neutral territory.

If the jump looks even, the ball will be deflected within the restraining circle and a scrimmage play may follow. In this case, look for the best opening into which to clear before tossing the ball, then back out fast with elbows spread for protection. Anticipation of control, direction and prompt clearance come with experience.

Failure to Jump: If a player refuses to jump, he must remain in position until the ball is tapped. The jumper often collides with the non-jumper upon landing. The jumper should not be penalized for charging on this play, unless there is evident intent to foul. Players do incline slightly forward in jumping but the deflection of the ball by opposing hands usually straightens them up.

Where there is negligible contact, it is up to you to distinguish between a slight nudge that had no bearing on the jump and one that did.

Stalling: If one jumper is taking more time than necessary to set for the jump, toss the ball for the ready jumper. The fact that the ready jumper will completely control the tap will stop further stalling. It isn't necessary to call a foul too hastily for delay; neither is it advisable to call time-out to warn the staller.

If, after you toss the ball for the ready jumper, the staller takes a running start and leaps, call a violation for an illegal jump. Both these methods will defeat the staller.

There is another type of staller who will deliberately withhold the ball to delay the game. Instead of handing the ball to the nearer official, he will stop to chat with teammates, give meaningless directions, or toss the ball to the farther official. If the offense is flagrant or if it is repeated after a warning, call a technical foul. Make certain that such fouls are called only when the stalling tactics consume more than the usual time for a jump. Officials should never delay in controlling the jump.

Tricks: To overcome a height advantage, the shorter jumper may wrist-slap his taller opponent, step on his feet, or raise his

Fouls on Jump Balls. Shown here are two common tricks that are used by small players to steal the tap from taller opponents. Above, resting forearm on opponent's chest on the way up. At right, holding left hand over opponent's jumping arm before the tap.

arm in the path of the big fellow's arm to prevent a controlled tap. These are personal fouls.

The player who feigns a dash for the tap, then blocks out the opposing jumper is also committing a foul.

When officiating alone, shoot quick glances right and left after toss-ups to catch any pushing fouls by other players. These fouls go unnoticed when the single official concentrates too much on the jumpers.

Reminders: Before tossing, warn the players occasionally with such friendly remarks as "Jump clean, boys," "Keep it open," and "Steady." This often forestalls fouls.

When you see unnecessary crowding, step in between the jumpers, separate them with your elbows, then step back promptly and toss. At other times, you may delay the toss a moment until the jumpers respond to your order to separate.

Don't anticipate held balls. The rule definitely states that "there must be a tug at the ball, and that players must have one or both hands so firmly on the ball that neither can gain sole possession."

A held ball should be called when a closely guarded player is *withholding the ball from play* and making no effort to put the ball into play. When a player is cornered, give him reasonable time to release the ball, then call a jump. Teasing tactics by the offensive player, who can stretch and pivot for an unlimited time, only lead to roughness.

SHOOTING

Many players intentionally shoot underhand to draw hacking fouls. The guard, expecting an orthodox overhand shot, makes an honest attempt at the ball. But the shooter, with an upward release, contacts his arm. Do not call a foul for hacking unless the guard definitely makes a "hacking" movement.

Striking the Hand: If, in blocking a shot or pass, or in securing the ball from an opponent, a player strikes the ball and at the same time touches the opponent's hand with his hand, no other contact taking place, the contact is *not* considered a foul. Too many officials disregard this rule and penalize the player on the grounds that the arm was hit. This call shows either ignorance, blindness, or lack of courage.

Holding: If, in your opinion, the guard held the shooter's arms as he attempted to shoot, you may call for two free throws. The ball need not necessarily leave the shooter's hands.

Charging: A guard will often make a remarkable interception of a shot with his hand, then hit the shooter with the rest of his body. Most spectators only see the hand that sensationally stops the ball. They'll howl, but call a foul for charging.

Fouling the Shooter: Watch the guard to see he doesn't charge the shooter after the release of the ball (like roughing the kicker in football). Some officials ignore this play, because the shot has been released, or miss it because they are watching the flight of the ball. A foul should be called, since the shooter is still considered in the act of shooting. If the shooter is fouled after he has regained his equilibrium, it is only one free throw.

The following play has caused some confusion: An "A" player leaps forward to take a looped shot. The "B" player holds his position and makes an honest attempt at the ball. "A" shoots and, as his momentum carries him forward, lands upon "B." This is a foul on "A" for charging. "A" had no right to charge "B" as the latter stood his ground; "A" caused the contact. "A" should have stopped to take his shot, or attempted to go around "B."

On the other hand, if "B" *stepped forward,* leaped and contacted "A," then "B" is charged with a foul, since he was not in an effective position to stop the shot from his original spot.

It is possible that "A" and "B" may contact each other from favorable positions. In this case contact is unavoidable and no foul is charged.

Anticipating Baskets: Do not blow the whistle in anticipation of a sure basket, only to find the ball has rolled off the hoop. Some officials shout "keep playing" after the whistle; this is wrong, because the whistle stops play. Call a jump ball at the foul line. It is not necessary to blow the whistle when a goal is scored.

"A goal is scored, whether made or not, if an opponent inter-

Hooking leg on free throw. The white-shirted player under the basket secures an illegal advantage on the rebound by hooking his opponent's leg.

feres with the ball, net or basket while the ball is on the hoop or within the basket. If an offensive player interferes at his own basket, it is no goal whether made or not, but a jump ball between centers at near foul line."

THE FREE THROW

In supervising the foul shot (a chore of the trailing official), check the set-up, then drop back to the rear at least six feet to the left of the shooter. This proximity to the side line enables you to clear to your working territory immediately after the ball is released.

Many officials stand too close to the shooter, possibly disconcerting him, or get run over when there is a change in possession and a fast break.

The leading official should be at his observation post to the right of the basket, and never directly underneath, where he may disconcert the shooter.

Remind the boys about taking their proper positions. "Watch

the lines, boys" and "Arms down" admonitions will usually be heeded by them, as they realize they will be penalized if they ignore these hints. It isn't necessary for an official to assume a detective attitude ("Ah, I caught your toes over the line, *no basket!*"). If the players disregard the friendly hints, give your decision with added emphasis.

Do not give the ball to the shooter until there is a legal set-up in the lanes. If the shooter already has the ball, hold him off until the players are ready.

Check "jockeying" for position in the lanes. Permit the taller of the two defensive players to select either visiting area and *remain* there. The others fill in. On courts where the visiting and home areas are not marked, it is a simple matter to chalk-mark the approximate distances.

Do not permit disconcerting actions by defensive players such as knee bobbing, arm raising, pointing, or unnecessary talking. If the shot is made, ignore these actions. If missed, however, give the shooter another try. These disconcerting actions should be nipped at the start.

The leading official watches the players, while the trailing official takes the lines and flight of the ball. The single official should not concentrate on the ball; he should cover the action with split vision.

Some of the known fouls that occur after a foul shot attempt are: (1) Lifts, where a player rests on an opponent's back or shoulder to use him as a springboard or to keep him down. (2) Holding a player's belt or stepping on his shoes. (3) Elbowing a player out of position. (4) Body pushing an opponent out of the path of the rebound while raising arms to feign an honest attempt. (5) Hand pushing.

Clearance: Delay in clearing may also cause interference with the play. Whether the foul try is made or missed, the official in charge of the shot must glide promptly to the nearer side line, facing the play as he clears. In this observation post, he is in excellent position to cover the ensuing action or to break ahead as play indicates.

The leading official glides around the boundary line the moment the ball comes in possession of the opposite basket. He should not turn his back on the throw-in after the foul is made. He lingers momentarily between the end line and foul line to supervise the throw-in. No handling of the ball is required. At the same time, he must see there is no interference by the team that scored, such as batting the ball away to delay the throw. The latter is a technical foul.

MISCELLANEOUS

Push-off: Call a pushing foul on the offensive player who pushes aside his opponent on the get-away.

Force-out: Call a "force out" only when the players are close to the out-of-bounds lines and there is a negligible amount of contact. When a player is pushed two and three feet from the lines, it is a foul.

Kicking: Kicking the ball is a violation only when it is a positive act.

Offensive Twist: Determine the cause of certain contacts; e.g., "A" and "B" tug at the ball; "B," in his honest attempt, slides down the arms or body of "A," who caused this by a quick twist, tug, and turn.

The hasty official calls a holding foul on "B" before the latter has time to recover his balance. This is wrong as "B" made no attempt to hold, and removed his arms from "A" as quickly as he could. If reasonable time were given "B" to recover from his unfavorable position, and he still held, then the official would be justified in calling "B" for holding.

Chapter 7

OFFICIATING ON NON-REGULATION COURTS

BASKETBALL IS PLAYED wherever there is room for two baskets. It is played in cellars, schools, churches, auditoriums, and various recreation halls. The following conditions may be encountered:

1. *Low Ceiling court:* Here you will find the offense driving hard for close-in shots and the defense ganging up, causing many jump balls and much body contact.

2. *Narrow court:* A defensive game is the rule here with many out-of-bounds plays and popular use of the zone defense.

3. *Seats or stands* practically on the boundary lines make throw-ins difficult, limit your clearance area, and cause difficulty on many out-of-bounds decisions.

4. *Baskets attached to the walls* make cutting past the basket impossible. The insufficient playing area behind the basket forces you to be on the spot every time the ball or player contacts the wall. Usually, "home-ground" rules are necessary. This situation also causes "gang-up" play on rebounds.

5. *A slippery floor:* Where players keep sliding and you must judge intent to avoid penalizing unavoidable skidding.

6. The *three-second rule* further handicaps the offense, because of the limited territory from the parallel foul lanes to the side lines.

7. The *ten-second (center) line* may not be at least 40 feet from the end line, causing forced front-court play and a pressing defense.

To the schools and coaches, the author recommends the hiring of a veteran official who knows his job thoroughly. Because of the court's limitations, one official may be used instead of two.

It may be wise to waive the three- and ten-second rules on these non-regulation courts. There are so many odd-sized courts that it may be worthwhile for the rules makers to draft some legislation or offer suggestions.

Veteran officials who have worked under these conditions may not need the advice that follows; young officials may study them with benefit.

1. Attempt to stay slightly behind the play.

2. If necessary to avoid interference, squeeze in among the spectators.

3. Make your working area as close to the side lines as possible.

4. Don't cross the court for an out-of-bounds play. Use the "pitch-and-drop-back-to-same" side method. Of course it will be necessary to cross on jump balls, but be sure your back is to the nearer side line.

5. In handling throw-ins on your side, remain ahead of play or slightly behind, according to where you were at the time of the whistle. This is to avoid interfering with the throw-ins. In either case, after the pass is made by the thrower, get into the best available position to observe the ensuing action.

6. On jump balls, back out quickly and get *behind* the play as soon as possession is indicated, to avoid being in the way of potential receivers.

7. Take your observation post about on line with the back of the foul circle, instead of on the foul line extended.

8. Don't be too technical on the throw-ins if you feel the thrower is making an honest effort. He may occasionally step in because of the lack of space to set his feet or arms.

9. Many home-court rules permit a *free* throw-in to avoid continual delay in keeping the guard back three feet. This throw-in cannot be deflected by the guard playing the thrower, but may be intercepted by the four other defensive players.

10. On a slippery floor, allow for unintentional sliding if the ball-handler makes an honest attempt to avoid "dragging" after a stop.

11. Notify the boys to play the whistle and not take close line plays for granted.

12. Do not call fouls on suspicion; they must be evident.

13. Give special attention to all rebounds. Do not suppress aggressive play. The players should be given a fair opportunity to gain control of the ball regardless of crowded conditions. Too many officials call a jump as soon as two opponents touch the ball.

14. Do not guess on out-of-bounds plays. If you miss one admit it and call for a jump. Appeal to the spectators' sportsmanship if they delight in kicking or batting the out-of-bound ball back to the court. You may miss a few plays on a congested court, but with experience you'll avoid being screened.

On some out-of-bounds plays you miss, the teams will commit themselves. They will line up quickly, anticipating a correct call from you. If you see this, it is reasonably safe to let the play ride; call it after a delayed split-second. However, a late whistle is bad. Don't let this happen if you can help it. There are "actors" who, noticing the delay, will pretend the ball belongs to their side. If you're working with a partner and one of you misses a play, he should look to the other official for a sign. The latter should demonstrate or point. If both of you miss the play, call a jump ball.

These suggestions, of course, are to be followed only under non-regulation court conditions.

Chapter 8

DO'S AND DON'TS

DO'S

1. Get a medical check-up before and during the season.
2. Study the rules carefully and practice the code of signals.
3. Answer all offers immediately.
4. Keep a date book of assignments and various directions to schools.
5. Attend frequent interpretation meetings, clinics, and the like.
6. Apply for membership in a recognized Board of Officials organization
7. Discuss your problems with experienced officials.
8. Get sufficient experience in minor games before attempting to officiate major ones.
9. Wear a uniform distinct from that of either team. If there is no Board of Officials' regulation outfit, the best colors are gray or white and black striped shirt, with gray trousers.
10. Be neat and well groomed.
11. Use discretion in all your actions. Remember you are in the public eye and set an example to the players as to language, conduct, etc.
12. Keep playing secrets of teams to yourself.
13. Arrive early to study surrounding conditions. Some non-regulation courts may have special rulings on fixtures, apparatus, low ceiling, over-crowding or other irregularities.
14. After dressing, relax for a half hour before starting time.

Pat Kennedy, a truly great official, in action. At the top he is shown withholding the ball until his out-of-bounds decision is clearly understood by both sides. Below, calling a foul. There is no doubt as to who committed it on whom and the number of shots awarded.

15. Check your valuables with a responsible person.
16. Consult the coaches as to time allowed for practice.
17. Check or supervise the checking of the ball for regulations and air pressure.
18. Keep the ball in your possession before the game and between the halves; return it to the proper authorities at the end of the game.
19. Give yourself sufficient time to check with scorers and timers before the game, regarding line-ups, signals, etc.
20. Introduce the opposing captains and explain any special rulings.
21. Always give the player the benefit of doubt.
22. Be firm, but conduct yourself in a kindly and friendly manner so that you will not antagonize the players.
23. Be consistent. The first foul is just as important as the last.
24. Be businesslike. Render your decisions clearly and decisively, using common sense and good judgment at all times.
25. Where time restrictions are involved, count to yourself; 1000-and-1, 1000-and-2, 1000-and-3, etc., so that timing will be accurate. In the 10-second play, count aloud from *6 on* if ball has not been brought from back to front court. At home you should test accuracy in timing against a stop watch.
26. Warn players or occasionally remind them about line or other infractions to forestall fouls or violations.
27. Run in neutral territory. In the double-referee system, run on the outside, parallel to lines. In the single-official game, run on the inside.
28. Dash in quickly for toss-ups and keep your back to the nearer side line.
29. Co-operate with the other official. Don't try to outdo him.
30. On time-outs, mentally record whose possession, spot play ceased, opposing jumpers (by number also) if a held ball, etc.
31. If there is a tendency toward roughness, stop the game and give the teams a warning. An appeal to their sportsmanship may help.

Indiscriminate use of the hands is a popular form of fouling that should be discouraged at the outset. The dark-shirted player guarding the rebounder under the basket in the top picture, and the white-shirted man guarding the pivot-post player in the bottom picture are both guilty of "hands." A slight pressure in either instance will throw the offensive man off balance.

32. Be sure you understand the spirit of the rule as well as its practical application.
33. Distinguish between an insignificant nudge that does no damage and the slightest push that does.
34. A sharp blast of the whistle, a prompt signal to the table officials, a snappy statement of your decision, and a rapid deployment to the proper station, sums up the call.
35. If your decision is a foul:
    a) Give time-out signal immediately.
    b) Announce the nature of the foul, stating who did what to whom.
    c) Call and hand-signal fouling player's number.
    d) Announce the number of free throws awarded.
    e) Proceed quickly to foul line.
36. If your decision is a held ball:
    a) Signal thumbs up.
    b) Secure ball quickly.
    c) Designate the jumpers and rush in for the toss. Throw the ball higher than the taller jumper can leap.
37. If your decision is a violation or out of bounds:
    a) Signal and clearly state the play.
    b) Designate the offensive player nearest spot to put ball in play, assisting by pointing toward the possessors' basket.
    c) Toss ball snappily to offensive player if it is a front-court throw-in.
    d) Do not handle ball on back-court throw-in.
38. Control the ball completely before handing or tossing it to a player on a front-court out-of-bounds throw-in. Do not be content just to touch the ball, in case the player has already taken possession.
39. If your partner sees an outside ball the other way, call a toss-up nearest the spot between two evenly matched opponents.
40. Where there is confusion on outside balls, keep the ball dead until both teams have understood the decision and are properly lined up.

The defensive man is fouling a legitimately moving screener to get at the shooter. Since the screener was more than three feet from the guard and was moving away from him, the onus for contact is on the guard.

Blocking or Charging? Or both? The official must determine whether the cutter has attempted to run over his man, whether the latter has deliberately blocked his path, or whether both offenses were committed.

41. If you miss an outside ball, look for a quick sign from the other official. If he lets you down or has also missed the play, call a jump nearest the spot. Don't guess.
42. Suggest dismissal of table officials if they prove inefficient or unscrupulous. They may be guilty of unsportsmanlike conduct such as:
    a) Blowing the horn at the wrong time to confuse the players.
    b) Cutting or over-running time.
    c) Erasing or charging personal fouls to the wrong players. Make certain of their guilt. The rules cover irregularities or disagreements.
43. Check with scorers and timers at the end of the half.
44. Notify the timers to call the teams three minutes before the intermission is over.
45. In accepting substitutes, walk toward the incoming players, receive them, point or introduce to proper opponents, then resume game promptly.
46. Be on the alert for a scrap. You may often prevent it with tactful advice or a humorous remark.
47. Be sure to notify the teams if they have exhausted their time-outs.
48. During the time-outs notify the captains as to the time left to play, if the gym has no electric timer.
49. Relay the numbers of the players committing fouls, time-outs, etc., to the scoring table (nearer official).
50. Remain with one team during time-outs. Permit players to leave the court for a drink of water, so that the court will be kept dry.
51. Cover all ball-handling situations as quickly as possible, especially near the end when time is precious to the losers. Nothing makes an official appear more incompetent as his inability to cope with stalling tactics, unnecessary jockeying for position, and other delays.
52. If both you and your partner blow your whistles on a play, the umpire should hold off a split-second until the referee announces his decision. It may be the same call. If different

decisions are given, such as a held ball and a foul, the foul takes preference.

DON'TS

1. Don't attempt to officiate when you're ill. Notify the proper authorities in time for a replacement.
2. Don't decline a game because you think it will be too tough or withdraw from an assignment to accept a better offer.
3. Don't work cut-rate. There are standard fees for high schools, colleges, etc.
4. Don't accept an entire schedule for a special fee.
5. Don't officiate too often for the same team, or you may be labeled a "homer."
6. Don't boast about your being in demand.
7. Don't trade games with other officials if you both coach on the side. This creates suspicion.
8. Don't become involved in long discussions with coaches.
9. Don't "coast" to conserve energy for another game.
10. Don't second guess the losing coach or glorify the winner.
11. Don't anticipate fouls, only the direction of play.
12. Don't always watch the ball; use split vision.
13. Don't lack the courage of your convictions.
14. Don't be afraid to call the fourth personal (disqualifying) foul on a "star."
15. Don't permit players to act up (e.g.—The player who puts his hand on his head and gives you that "who, me?" look, or uses other unsportsmanlike gestures).
16. Don't act up yourself; dramatics are unnecessary. (The crowd came to see the game, not you.)
17. Don't be officious or assert your authority too strongly.
18. Don't be swayed by partisan coaches or biased crowds.
19. Don't try to apologize or atone for mistakes. You're not infallible.
20. Don't adopt a smug know-it-all attitude.
21. Don't embroider your decisions; signal promptly to avoid confusion.
22. Don't let up because the game is one-sided.

23. Don't wait for a field goal to settle a tie; call fouls to the very end.
24. Don't penalize unavoidable contact where the players were in favorable positions.
25. Don't penalize clean hard play; distinguish between roughness and aggressiveness.
26. Don't let the other official carry the entire load.
27. Don't chat with players, coaches, or spectators during the game.
28. Don't explain or alibi a decision to the "bench" during a time-out.
29. Don't announce a decision with the whistle in your mouth.
30. Don't carry the whistle in your mouth. In a collision you may break your teeth or cut your lips.
31. Don't keep alibi-ing to the other official, "Sorry, I missed the play."
32. Don't be sensitive when the other official has to cover you on some calls.
33. Don't infringe on the other official's territory unless it is necessary.
34. Don't lose your poise when working the side on which the players' benches are situated.
35. Don't delay the game by lining up the players at every substitution, unless many enter at once and you feel it is necessary. In this case, line them up at the spot where play ceased.
36. Don't put the ball into play following a time-out, until the opposing captains have acknowledged the ready-signal.
37. Don't call "phantom" fouls because you feel you are not earning your fee. Your ability is rated by your judgment and the manner in which you control the game and not by the number of fouls you call.
38. Don't fail to call violations on players who step inside the restraining circle before the ball has been tapped on a jump. Unless you stop it at the very beginning, the players will keep offending.
39. Don't shift most of the responsibility to the other official; shoulder your share of the load.

INDEX

Anticipating goal, 58

Bucket situations, 33, 34, 38

Clearance, 19, 53, 55, 60
Conditioning, 1, 2
Counting seconds, 14, 15, 52
Courage, 5, 6, 10

Diet, 4
Dribbling, 39

Foot care, 4
Force-out, 61
Fouls:
  causes, 12
  types—
    accidental, 43
    blocking, 42, 45, 57
    charging, 42, 43, 45, 58
    face guarding, 52
    hacking, 57
    holding, 58
    kicking, 45
    pushing, 45, 61
    second guessing, 43
    technical, 52, 55
Fumbling, 43

Handling ball:
  free-throw, 59, 60, 61
  jump ball, 53, 55, 57
  throw-in, 45, 48, 52

Interfering with basket, 58, 59

Kicking the ball, 61

Noisy crowd, 9
Non-regulation courts, 62, 63

Out-of-bounds, 45

Pivoting, 40, 42

Qualifications, 1

Ratings, 7
Rebounds, 43, 60
Relationship:
  with coach, 8
  with players, 8, 9
  with spectators, 9

Screening, 29, 33
Shower, 4, 5
Sleep, 5
Split vision, 3
Stalling, 52, 55
Stance, 19, 21, 53
Suggestions to officials:
  do's and don'ts, 65-73
  regarding non-regulation courts, 63-64

Unavoidable contacts, 45
Uniform, 2
Uniformity, 10, 11

Violations:
  cupping ball, 40
  dribbling, 40, 42
  jump ball, 55
  throw-in, 52
  toddling, 42
  traveling, 38, 42

Whistle, 3, 13
Working area:
  double-official system, 24-28
  of the single official, 16, 17
Worry, 5

NOTES

NOTES

NOTES

NOTES

NOTES

NOTES

NOTES

NOTES

Date Due
JAN 18 '91
APR 29 2001
'51
9